Five Children and It

A classic story by E Nesbit

Adapted by Gill Munton

Series Editor: Louis Fidge

Contents

CHAPTER 1

The sand fairy

Cyril and his brothers and sisters were on their way to the White House. They were going to spend the summer there. The children's mother was with them, but their father had to stay in London. He had some important work to do in his office.

'Here we are!' said Mother.

The children looked at the White House. The house stood on a hill. There were lots of flowers in the garden, and they could see fruit trees, too. There was a wood behind the house.

'Come on!' said Robert. 'Let's explore!' Robert was the younger of the two boys. He loved adventures, and he was always looking forward to the next one.

Anthea, Cyril, Robert and Jane jumped out of the pony cart and ran into the garden. Mother followed. She carried Baby in her arms.

Life at the White House was very different from life in London. There were trees, and woods, and flowers, and green, green grass. Every day, there was a new place to explore, and the five children were very happy. But they missed their father.

One day, Mother received a letter.

When she had read it, she said, 'Children, your grandmother is not well. I must go and look after her. I must go straight away.'

'What about us?' asked Jane. 'Who will look after *us*?' Jane was the youngest child, and she didn't want her mother to go away.

'Martha, of course.' Martha was the children's nursemaid. 'You must all be very good and do what she says.'

After breakfast the next day, Cyril said, 'Let's take our spades, and dig in the big sand pit behind the fruit trees. We can pretend we are at the seaside.' Cyril was the eldest, and he liked to take charge of his brothers and sisters.

So off they went to the sand pit. Each child carried a spade, and they took it in turns to carry Baby.

First, they built a sandcastle. But it wasn't much fun, because there was no sea water to rush in through the door and wash it away.

Then Cyril said, 'I know what we can do! Let's dig a great big hole! If we make it deep enough, we might get to Australia!'

So they picked up their spades and started to dig.

Baby wanted to eat some sand.

'He thinks it's sugar!' said Anthea. Anthea was the second eldest child. She was very fond of Baby, and looking after him made her feel grown up.

They dug, and they dug, until they were hot and covered in sand. The hole was very deep.

'Let's stop now!' said Jane. 'If we *do* get to Australia, the Australian children will get sand in their eyes!' She went to explore a little cave with Robert and Cyril.

Anthea knew that Australia was still a long way away, and she carried on digging.

Suddenly, Anthea said, 'Cyril! Robert! Jane! Look what I've found! Oh! I think it's alive! Come on, before it runs away!'

The children ran back to the hole and looked in.

'I can see a foot,' said Anthea. 'And fur!'

'Maybe it's a rat,' said Robert.

'It's much bigger than a rat!' said Anthea. 'And it hasn't got a … oh! It said something! I'm sure it did!' She started to dig with her hands.

Then they heard a hoarse, grumpy voice. 'I said, leave me alone!'

The children looked at each other in astonishment. Then Anthea said, 'We want to see you. We wish you would come out!'

Two big, pointed ears poked up from the sand at the bottom of the hole, followed by the rest of the creature. It had a round, furry body, and furry arms and legs. Its hands and feet were like a monkey's. But the strangest thing was its eyes. They were on the end of long horns, like a snail's eyes.

'What is it?' said Jane. 'Can we take it home?'

The creature turned its eyes to look at her. 'Take me home? Of course you can't take me home, you silly girl!'

'Don't be angry,' said Anthea. 'It's just that – well, we don't know who you are. Will you tell us?'

'I'm a sand fairy, of course.'

'How long have you lived here?' asked Robert.

'Oh, about a thousand years! Sand fairies used to live by the sea. People sent their children to ask us for wishes. One wish a day. It lasted until sunset.'

'Do you still give people wishes?' asked Anthea.

'Of course I do! I gave you a wish two minutes ago.'

'No, you didn't.'

'I did! You said, "We wish you would come out" – and I did.'

'Oh, yes. Well – can we have another wish? Please?'

'All right – but be quick. I want to go back to sleep.'

But no one could think of a wish. Then Anthea remembered something she and Jane had wished for last summer.

'I wish – we were all very beautiful!' she said.

The sand fairy pushed out his eyes as far as they would go, and held his breath. His body grew much fatter, until it almost filled the hole. Suddenly, he let out his breath and went back to his normal size. Then he scratched at the sand with his monkey hands – and disappeared!

Anthea turned to speak to the others. But they had gone! All she could see was three beautiful children, with shining hair and large, sparkling eyes.

At first, no one spoke. Then Cyril said, 'Anthea! It's you! I can see your dirty handkerchief! You forgot to change it after you cut your finger. And you're Jane – I remember that hole in your dress!'

'Cyril!' said Anthea. 'Is that handsome young man really you?'

They all laughed.

'How beautiful we are!' said Jane. 'When we get home, Martha will think we are the most beautiful children in the world!'

Anthea went to pick up Baby, who was asleep on a heap of sand. He still looked like Baby. *Perhaps he is too young to have a wish,* thought Anthea.

But when Baby saw her, he frowned, and put a sandy finger in his mouth.

'Come to Anthea, darling!'

Baby started to cry.

'He doesn't know who I am!' said poor Anthea. 'He wants his big sister back!'

Baby cried and wriggled all the way home. When they reached the White House, Martha ran out. She looked very worried.

'Give me that baby!' she shouted. She snatched Baby from Anthea. 'Who are you? Where are my children?'

'We're *us*, of course!' said Cyril. 'Anthea, Jane, Robert, and me, Cyril! Please let us in, Martha! We're hungry!'

But Martha just glared at them, and slammed the door.

'We'll have to wait until sunset,' said Cyril. 'The wish only lasts for a day.'

So they sat on the grass near the White House. They waited for sunset. They were hungry, and cross, and tired – and a little frightened.

'We shouldn't have wished for beauty,' said Anthea. 'It's made things worse, not better.'

After a while, the children fell asleep. When Anthea woke up, it was almost dark. She looked at the others. Oh, thank goodness – they were back to normal. Not exactly ugly – but not beautiful, either.

'Wake up!' she cried.

When Martha saw them, she was cross again.

'Where have you been, you naughty children? It's nearly dark! I've been so worried about you.'

'We're very sorry, Martha. But it's not our fault,' said Anthea. 'They wouldn't let us come home until sunset.'

'Who wouldn't?'

'The beautiful children.'

'They came here!' said Martha. 'I sent them away!'

'We'll never play with them again, Martha. We promise.'

Then Cook came in. She was carrying a big plate of cold beef, and soon everyone was happy again.

CHAPTER 2

Pockets full of gold

In the morning, Jane said, 'I had a very strange dream last night. I dreamed that we met a sand fairy!'

'I dreamed that we met a sand fairy, too!' said Robert.

'And so did I!' said Anthea.

Then they heard Cyril's voice. 'We mustn't be late for breakfast!'

Cyril appeared in the doorway of the nursery, and Anthea said, 'Cyril – we all dreamed that we met a sand fairy!'

'It wasn't a dream!' laughed Cyril. 'We *did* meet a sand fairy. He gave us a wish, but it went wrong. That's why I want to make an early start this morning. We'll go and see the sand fairy again, and make another wish. But we must think about it more carefully this time.'

As they were eating breakfast, Jane said, 'Martha is taking Baby to see her sister today. We can go to the sand pit when they've gone.'

So after breakfast, they waved to Martha (in her best blue hat) and Baby (in his best white coat) as the pony cart clattered away. Then they set off for the sand pit. As they walked, they decided what to wish for.

'Humph!' said the sand fairy, as he brushed sand from his ears. 'So there you are! I thought you were a dream. I suppose you'd like a wish?'

'Yes, please! And we'd like a little extra one, too,' said Robert.

'We'll do the little extra one first,' said the sand fairy.

'We wish – that Martha wouldn't notice our wishes,' said Robert. 'It's very – inconvenient.'

'And the big wish?'

'We wish – for lots and lots of gold coins!' said Robert.

'Will a sand pit full be enough?'

'Oh, yes!'

'Then get out of the way!'

The children climbed out of the sand pit, and ran as fast as they could. When they stopped and looked back, they were dazzled by the sight. The sand pit was completely full of glittering, gleaming gold.

At first, they just played with the coins. They picked up handfuls of them, and let them run through their fingers. The coins made a wonderful noise.

Then Cyril said, 'Remember – our wish will only last until sunset. Let's fill our pockets, and go and spend some of our money.'

The coins were heavy, and they had to put some back. But they were soon on the road to Rochester.

When they arrived, they were hot and thirsty.

'I'm going first' Cyril said.

Cyril went into a shop to buy some lemonade. When he came out, he looked very cross.

'The man in the shop wouldn't take my gold coins. He laughed at them! I had to pay for the lemonade with my own money. And I only had two shillings and seven pence!'

They drank the lemonade, and then Anthea said, 'I'm the next oldest. It's my turn to buy something. I think I'll buy – a new hat.'

In the hat shop, Anthea chose a hat with pink roses on it. She held out three gold coins. But the lady said, 'I can't take those. Shops don't take money like that any more.'

It was the same everywhere. The children tried to buy a purse, toys and books. But none of the shopkeepers wanted the gold coins, so they couldn't buy anything.

Then Cyril saw a sign:

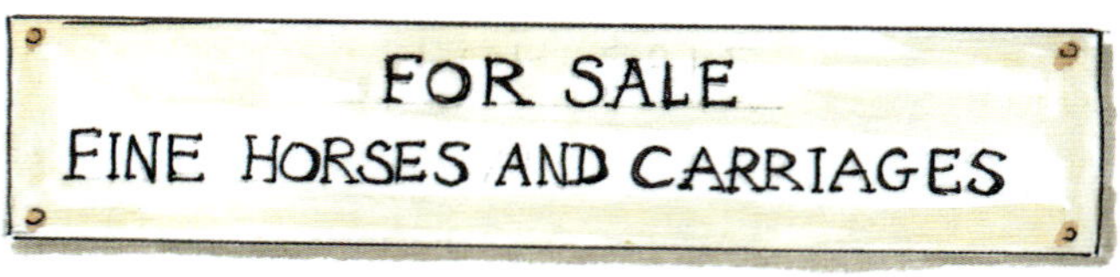

'Let's try one more time,' he said, and went into the stable yard.

A tall man was filling a bucket with water.

'Good morning!' said Cyril. 'I want to buy a horse and a carriage. Will you show me some, please? Then I can choose.'

The man looked at Cyril, and smiled. Then he started to laugh. 'How much money have you got?'

Robert didn't like it when the man laughed at Cyril. Angrily, he pulled out a handful of gold coins and showed them to the man.

The man snatched the coins, and stared at them for a moment. Then he called to his stable boy.

'William! Go and get the police! And close the gate behind you!'

While they were waiting for the police, the man said, 'Now, where did you get these gold coins?'

Jane was a very truthful girl.

'We got them from a fairy,' she said. 'A fairy who lives in a sand pit. He's got brown fur, and long ears, and eyes like a snail's – and he gives us a wish every day!'

'The poor child!' the man said, and he looked at Jane sadly. 'You children should be ashamed. You made your sister help you to steal – when she's not right in the head!'

Then a policeman arrived, and the tall man told his story.

'We'll take them to the police station,' said the policeman. 'You bring the girls, and I'll bring the boys.'

The children were angry and ashamed. As they walked, their eyes filled with tears. When Robert accidentally bumped into someone, he didn't know who she was.

Then a well-known voice said, 'Master Robert! Oh, what have you done now?'

It was Martha, with Baby in her arms!

As they walked, the policeman and the man from the stable yard told Martha about the gold coins. Baby started to cry.

People stopped and looked at them as they walked through the town.

'Empty your pockets,' Martha whispered to Robert, while the two men were talking to a lady in a big hat. 'I want to know the truth!'

Robert put his hands in his pockets and pulled out handfuls of gold coins. But of course, because of the little extra wish, Martha couldn't see them.

'These children haven't stolen anything!' she cried. 'They're good children!'

'We'll see,' said the policeman.

In the police station, the children were taken to see an inspector.

'Empty your pockets!' he said. 'You first, boy!'

Now we're really in trouble, thought Cyril. He put his hands in his trouser pockets.

He stood quite still for a moment. Then he started to laugh. There was nothing there! His pockets were empty! He looked out of the window to check. Yes, it was quite dark. The sun had set, just in time!

Of course, Robert's pockets, and Anthea's, and Jane's were empty too.

The policeman looked puzzled. 'They've played a trick on me!' he said. 'But I don't know how.'

Martha said, 'I told you – there *are* no gold coins. You've made a big mistake.' She glared at the policeman and the inspector and the man from the stable yard. 'Come on, children!'

And she marched out of the police station, followed by Cyril, Anthea, Robert and Jane.

But when they got home, Martha was angry with them.

'You shouldn't have gone into Rochester by yourselves!' she said, and sent them straight to bed. So instead of pockets full of gold, or fine horses and carriages, they had nothing – not even any dinner.

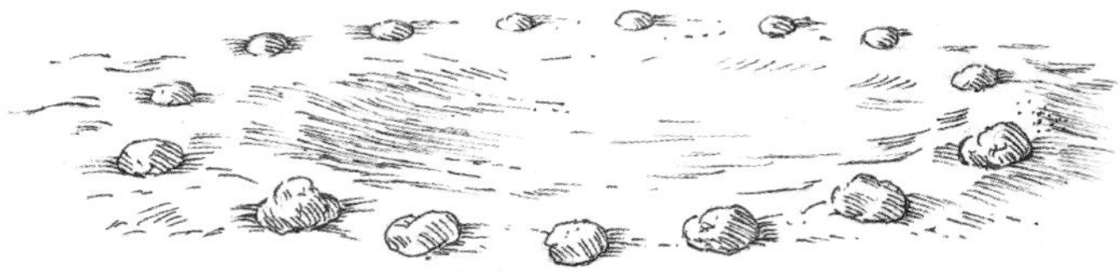

CHAPTER 3

Baby is stolen

They had tried being beautiful, and they had tried being rich, but these things had not made them happy. At breakfast the next morning, the children tried to talk seriously about their next wish. But Baby was being naughty.

He climbed out of his high chair.

He hit Cyril on the head with a spoon.

He put his hands in his bread and milk, and made a terrible mess.

He sang loudly, he banged his little feet on the table, and he knocked over a cup.

Finally, Baby pushed over the goldfish bowl. It rolled across the table. Water and goldfish poured out, and splashed onto the floor.

Martha mopped up the water, picked up the fish and put them back in the bowl. Then she took Baby upstairs to change his clothes. At last, the children could talk.

'Our first wish was silly,' Cyril said. 'As for our second wish – money would be more useful than gold. Let's wish for fifty pounds today.'

They set off for the sand pit.

But Martha ran after them.

'Don't forget Baby!' she said. She put him into Anthea's arms.

'Do we *have* to take him with us?' asked Robert. 'He's so naughty – we don't want him.'

'Of course you want him, the dear little thing!' replied Martha. 'Anyone would want him.'

Baby sat on Cyril's shoulders all the way to the sand pit. The others talked about what they would do with the fifty pounds.

But when they arrived, Anthea said, 'We didn't mark the place where the sand fairy lives! We don't know where to dig!'

They started to look for the sand fairy. They dug here, and they dug there, but they couldn't find him. After a while, they stopped to rest.

Baby was still being naughty. He snatched a handful of sand, and threw it in Anthea's face. Then he stuck his head in the sand and waved his fat little legs in the air. Of course, he got sand in his eyes, which made him cry. Robert used a bottle of lemonade to wash Baby's face.

'Martha was wrong,' he grumbled. 'It's not true that anyone would want him. Even *Martha* doesn't want him, not really. That's why she gave him to us. I wish people *would* want him. Then we might get some peace.'

There was silence. Then they heard, 'Good morning! Well, that was an easy one. Everyone wants Baby now.'

There was the sand fairy, sitting next to them.

'Robert didn't mean it!' said Jane. 'Please, can we wish for something else?'

'No, you can't,' replied the sand fairy. 'You must be very careful about what you wish for.'

Baby tried to grab the sand fairy, but he disappeared into the sand.

The children marked the place with a circle of stones.

'Now we'll know where to find him tomorrow,' said Robert.

On the way home, they met a horse and carriage. The lady inside the carriage was very grand. Her dress was made of white lace, with red ribbons. On her knee sat a little white dog, with a red ribbon round his neck.

When the lady saw Baby, she smiled and called out, 'What a dear little baby! Will you give him to me? I'll look after him very well. I am Lady Chittenden. He will have the best of everything.'

'You can't have him!' cried Anthea. 'He's ours!'

'May I hold him, then? Just for a minute.'

Lady Chittenden stepped down from her carriage. She wore red shoes, with high heels and shiny red buckles. Cyril put Baby into her arms.

Suddenly, Lady Chittenden jumped into the carriage and slammed the door.

'Drive on!' she called to the coachman. And the carriage clattered away.

The children looked at each other. Then they ran, as fast as they could, after the carriage. The little white dog was barking, and Baby was crying. But he stopped crying very soon, and the children knew he was asleep.

The carriage stopped at the gates of a grand house, and the children hid behind a hedge. Lady Chittenden stepped out of the carriage, and smiled down at Baby. He was asleep on the seat.

'I'm going to pick some flowers,' Lady Chittenden said to the coachman. 'I won't wake him, the dear little thing!'

Lady Chittenden went to pick some flowers.

'What a fine baby!' said the coachman to the footman. 'I wish he was mine! I think I'll hide him in the hedge, and tell Lady Chittenden that his brothers and sisters have taken him. Then I'll come back for him later.'

'Oh, no!' said the footman. 'I want that baby! You've got six children already!'

They were so busy quarrelling that they forgot about Baby.

Cyril crept up to the carriage and opened the door. He lifted Baby out, and carried him behind the hedge. Soon, the five children were on their way home.

But lots of other people saw Baby, and wanted him too.

A boy who was collecting firewood stared at Baby, and wanted to hold him.

A little girl followed them for a while, calling, 'Baby! Baby!'

A man stopped to tickle Baby's cheek.

'I'm glad it's nearly sunset,' said Cyril. 'Isn't it strange? Every day, we can't wait for our wish to end. It should be the other way round.'

At last, the sun set, and they went on their way without any more interruptions.

They were late for dinner, of course, and Martha was cross. But at least Baby was safe.

'You see,' said Robert, as they all kissed Baby goodnight. 'We *did* want him, after all.'

CHAPTER 4

Wings

Anthea woke up very early. She put on her clothes, and crept downstairs with her shoes in her hand. She had a plan, and she wanted to carry it out by herself.

She put on her shoes in the garden, and ran across the grass to the sand pit.

The sand fairy wasn't very pleased to see her.

'It's the middle of the night!' he grumbled. 'And it's so cold! I suppose you want a wish?'

'I want to talk to you,' said Anthea. 'Will you sit on my lap? It will keep you warm.'

'Thank you,' he said, and hopped onto Anthea's lap.

'I need your help,' began Anthea. 'We have had three wishes, and they have all gone wrong. Will you help us to wish for something more sensible next time?'

'I can't tell you what to wish for,' replied the sand fairy. 'The only advice I can give you is: think before you speak.'

'Well, I was thinking of wishing for wings,' said Anthea. 'Do you think that's a good idea?'

'You could wish for worse things,' said the sand fairy. He hopped off Anthea's lap, and disappeared into the sand.

Anthea was late for breakfast. When Martha wasn't looking, Robert picked up his spoon and poured some honey onto Baby's clothes. While Martha was cleaning him up, the other four children slipped out of the house.

On the way to the sand pit, Anthea said, 'I've had an idea about today's wish. I think we should wish for wings!'

'Wings would be lovely!' cried Jane. The boys liked the idea, too.

When they arrived at the sand pit, Anthea said to the sand fairy, 'I wish we all had wings, and could fly!'

The sand fairy puffed himself up, and the children's wings began to grow. They were like giant birds' wings, covered in soft, rainbow-coloured feathers.

Robert flapped his wings and jumped into the air.

'I can fly!' he cried, as he rose above the sand pit.

Soon, all four children were flying through the air. They flapped their wings and flew over the sand pit, and over the White House, and over Rochester …

Then Cyril said, 'All this flying has made me hungry.'

'I can see a plum tree,' said Jane. 'Let's fly down and eat some plums!'

They sat on a branch of the tree, and picked some plums.

As they flew away, they saw a horrified face looking up at them.

'That must be the owner of the plum tree,' said Anthea. 'I'll throw him some money to pay for the plums.'

'Don't be frightened!' she called. And she threw some money to the man.

But they were soon hungry again. They landed on top of a tall tower, and tried to decide what to do.

'We can't buy food from a shop,' said Anthea. 'People would be afraid of us. If we see some food, we'll just have to take it.'

'We flew past an open window a moment ago,' said Cyril. 'I could see lots of food on a shelf inside the room. There was cold chicken, and bread, and a bottle of lemonade.'

'All right,' said Anthea. 'But we must pay for what we take. Look in your pockets. See how much money you've got.'

Altogether, they had two shillings and sixpence.

They flew down to the open window. They took the chicken, the bread, and the bottle of lemonade, and left the money on the shelf.

Back at the top of the tower, they had a lovely picnic. When they had finished, they felt drowsy. Soon, all four children were asleep, wrapped in their soft, warm wings.

When they woke up, it was almost dark.

'Our wings have gone!' said Robert. 'It's after sunset!'

Cyril picked up the empty lemonade bottle. 'Well, flying was a lot of fun,' he said. 'Now we must go down and put this bottle back.'

But of course, they couldn't *fly* down.

'There's a little door here,' said Cyril. 'It must lead to some steps.'

He turned the door handle. But the door wouldn't move.

'It's locked!' said Robert.

The children looked at each other. Jane started to cry.

'I want to go home!' she wailed.

'Don't cry. We'll only be here for one night,' said Anthea, and put her arm round her sister. 'We can wave our handkerchiefs in the morning. Someone from the house will see them, and come and let us out.'

'And they will see the lemonade bottle, as well,' said Cyril. 'Then we'll be sent to prison for stealing.'

'Oh, let's just throw the bottle into the trees,' said Robert.

'What if it hits someone on the head?' asked Cyril. 'I'll hide it in my jacket. And then we must all shout – as loudly as we can.'

They had to shout for a long time before the front door of the house was opened. A man came out, and looked around him.

'Where are you?' he shouted.

'At the top of the tower!' replied Cyril.

'Come down, at once!'

'We can't – the door's locked!'

The man started to walk towards the tower. The children waited. Then they heard his voice on the other side of the door.

'How did you get up here?'

Cyril said, 'We climbed up the stairs – but then someone locked the door, and we were stuck.'

'I'm going to unlock it now,' said the man. 'But my wife tells me that someone has stolen some food from our house. If you are the thieves, I will call the police!'

But when he opened the door and saw them, he said, 'My goodness! You're just children! Come down, and tell me what happened.'

Soon, the children were sitting in a warm kitchen, drinking hot milk and eating cake.

'We fell asleep, you see,' explained Robert. 'When we woke up, someone had locked the door.'

'I locked it yesterday,' said the man. 'But who unlocked it, and then locked it again?'

'I don't know, sir.'

Then the man's wife looked hard at Cyril, and said, 'What have you got in your jacket, young man?'

Cyril pulled out the lemonade bottle.

'All right,' he said. 'We *did* take some food from your house. The window was open. But we left two shillings and sixpence to pay for it.'

'You still shouldn't have taken the food. And how did you get up to the window?' asked the man. 'It's very high.'

'We can't tell you that,' said Cyril.

There was a long silence.

Then the man said, 'Well, no harm has been done. And you *did* leave the money. I'll take you home now – it's very late.'

He stood up, and went to get his horse and cart.

This time, Martha was very cross, and she told them to stay indoors the next day as a punishment.

CHAPTER 5

The castle

'Just half an hour, Martha. Please! It's very important!' Martha looked at Robert, and then she looked at her watch.

'All right, Master Robert. You may go out for half an hour. But no more!'

It was a hot day, and the sand fairy was out of his hole. He turned to look at Robert.

'Where are the others?' he said. 'I hope they haven't had an accident with those wings.'

'No,' said Robert. 'But the wings did get us into trouble – just like all the other wishes. We have to stay in the house today, as a punishment. I have only been let out for half an hour. So can we do today's wish quickly, please?'

But he couldn't think of a wish. Toffee? A football? A penknife with three blades? No – they were just little things. And they were only for him, not for all of them.

'I can't think of a wish,' he told the sand fairy. 'I wish one of the others could choose – oh, no! I didn't mean it!'

But it was too late. The sand fairy was already puffing himself up.

Robert ran all the way home. He was sure that the others would wish for something silly. Pet mice, or chocolate …

But the White House had gone! In its place stood – a castle!

Robert rubbed his eyes. The castle was still there. One of the others must have wished for it! He walked closer, and saw knights in armour standing near the huge wooden gate. They were going to attack! One of the knights saw Robert, and walked towards him.

'What are you doing here, boy?' the knight asked. 'This is a dangerous place – there is going to be a battle.'

'I – I just want to go home!' said poor Robert.

'And where is home?'

'It's – here!'

'I must tell our leader, Sir Wulfric,' said the knight.

Sir Wulfric sat on a big, grey horse, and he wore a helmet with a red feather. He carried a long sword, and a shield with three red lions on it.

'Tell me why you are here, my boy,' he said kindly to Robert, as he took off his helmet. 'We will not hurt you.'

So Robert told him all about the sand fairy, and the gold coins, and the wings.

'So you see,' he said. 'You are here because of a wish.'

Sir Wulfric frowned.

'He's pretending to be mad!' said the knight. 'He thinks you will let him go if you believe he's mad!'

Sir Wulfric thought for a moment. Then he said, 'You have told me some strange things, my boy. But I have no reason to hurt you. You may go free. This is Jakin – he will go with you.'

Robert ran back to the sand pit as fast as he could. Jakin went with him.

'Just one more wish! Please!' he begged the sand fairy.

'Hurry up – I'm very tired,' the creature grumbled.

'What is the wish?'

'I wish I was with the others!' said Robert. As the sand fairy began to puff himself up, Robert closed his eyes.

When he opened his eyes, he was standing in a square room with thick stone walls. He was inside the castle!

Anthea, Cyril and Jane were surprised to see him. He told them his story, and Anthea said, 'You have been so brave. You can be our leader in the battle.'

'We haven't done anything yet,' Jane told him. 'But we are going to shoot at the knights through these narrow little windows. We can use the bow and arrows Uncle Richard gave you.'

'I don't think that will work,' Robert replied. 'They've got *real* bows and arrows, and swords, and daggers. Jakin told me that they will attack us just before sunset. Let's get ready. We can start by exploring the rest of the castle.'

So they explored. They wandered up and down stone steps, through archways, up and down towers, and through room after room after room.

After a while, they found themselves in a large garden. And there they saw the strangest sight.

In the middle of the garden stood Martha! Next to her stood Cook, who seemed to be holding something – but there was nothing in her hands. Baby was there, too – sitting on nothing, about a metre from the ground.

Anthea held out her arms to Baby. But Martha said, 'Leave him alone, Miss Anthea. Let him sit quietly in his high chair.'

Then Cook spoke.

'Run along and play, children. Or there won't be any dinner. I'm late already.'

The children went back into the castle.

'What's going on?' said Anthea. 'I don't like it. It's strange to see Martha and Cook and Baby in the castle.'

'I think I can explain it,' said Cyril slowly. 'You see, the castle is in the same place as the White House. We are in the castle, because we are in the wish. But Martha, and Cook, and Baby – they can't see the castle, because they are in the house. Remember – they can't see any of our wishes. And we can't see the chairs, or the dinner – because they are in the house, too.'

'Stop, Cyril!' cried Jane. 'My head is going round and round. All I know is, I'm hungry and I want my dinner. I hope *that* will be real!'

They watched Cook as she put an invisible pan into an invisible oven. After a while, Martha brought them an invisible tray. She started to carve an invisible leg of lamb with an invisible knife. As she served invisible potatoes and invisible cabbage with an invisible spoon, poor Jane started to cry.

CHAPTER 6

The knights attack

Cyril pushed his hand into his pocket and brought out three biscuits. They were broken and crumbly, but they were food. Cyril shared them out.

As they ate the biscuits, Robert said, 'We can see the biscuits but we couldn't see the leg of lamb. Why's that?'

Cyril thought for a moment. 'It must be because *we've* got them, and not Martha,' he said.

'Now,' said Robert. 'We'd better find out what's happening outside the castle.'

They all climbed to the top of a tower, and looked out of one of the narrow windows.

The knights were very busy now. They were sharpening their daggers, getting their bows ready, and polishing their shields. Cyril saw some horses dragging a huge tree trunk towards the castle. *That's a battering ram,* he thought. *They will try to break the door down with it. Thank goodness the castle has a moat, and the drawbridge is up.*

'We must defend the castle,' Cyril said. 'Just the four of us.'

'It's only a game, isn't it?' Jane asked.

But no one answered.

They went to search for weapons. There were plenty of swords and bows, but they were all too heavy for a child.

'We can throw these daggers,' said Cyril. 'They're much lighter. And I saw some stones in the courtyard. We can throw those as well, if they try to swim across the moat.'

While they were collecting the stones, they heard the sound of a trumpet.

'They're going to attack!' said Robert, and they all rushed to the window. 'Let's get ready to defend the castle!'

'You *are* brave, Robert,' said Anthea.

Cyril's face turned red. '*I'm* brave, too!' he said. 'I just wasn't ready.'

'Oh, I don't care which of you is braver!' cried Jane. 'We should never have wished for a castle! I hate this game! And I don't want to play!'

'It's all right,' said Anthea. 'They can't get in. And anyway, they wouldn't hurt women or children.'

They watched the knights move towards the castle. Then they heard a voice, far below them.

'In the name of our great leader, Sir Wulfric de Talbot, I order you to surrender!'

'Never!' shouted Robert in reply. The children cheered, and rattled their daggers.

It was getting dark outside. *Nearly sunset,* thought Jane.

Anthea had been thinking, too. 'The moat is very narrow,' she said. 'It must be easy to swim across it.'

'Even if they do swim across, they can't get in,' said Robert. But as he spoke, they heard heavy footsteps on the stairs, and the clanking of armour.

Robert opened the door and crept up the stairs.

'Wait here!' he whispered. He peeped into the little room at the top of the stairs. Jakin was there, dripping with moat water and bending over something. *The machine that works the drawbridge!* thought Robert. *It's in that room!*

As Jakin turned and rushed out at him, he banged the door shut and turned the big silver key.

Then he remembered the window. There was just one big window in the castle – big enough for a man to climb through.

'Quickly!' he called to the others, and they all ran to the room with the big window.

One of the knights was climbing through the window! Robert and Cyril pushed him, hard, and he fell back into the moat with a splash.

Then Robert and Cyril ran out of the room and locked the door.

The two boys looked at each other. They were breathing heavily.

Then they heard an enormous crash.

'It's the drawbridge!' cried Robert. 'It's down! I was too late!'

They heard the clatter of horses' hooves, and the sound of marching feet. The knights were crossing the drawbridge and coming into the castle!

'Quick!' shouted Robert. 'It's time to get the stones.'

The children dropped the stones through the narrow windows. They heard shouts from below as the stones landed on the knights.

'We won't surrender!' cried Robert as he picked up a big stone. 'Never!'

Then he heard the sound of the battering ram. The knights were trying to break down the castle door!

'Please let's wave a handkerchief and surrender!' begged Jane.

In answer to this, Robert looked round for something else to throw. He saw an iron pot full of water. He threw this out of the window, too.

Suddenly, the cries of the knights and the sounds of the horses grew fainter. The little room whirled round.

It was sunset!

The children ran to the window. The moat and the knights had gone. All they could see was the garden of the White House, with its marigolds and roses and iron railings.

'We didn't surrender, did we?' said Robert proudly.

'Are you glad we wished for a castle?' asked Cyril.

'I think so,' said Anthea slowly.

'Me too!' cried Jane. 'I wasn't frightened at all!'

Then Anthea said, 'All our other wishes have got us into trouble with Martha. But this one didn't, did it?'

But just as Anthea finished speaking, the nursery door flew open and Martha marched in.

'You should be ashamed of yourselves!' she said. 'Pouring water out of the window – just as I was cleaning the door knocker underneath! Now off to bed, all of you!'

'What were you saying, Anthea?' asked Cyril, when Martha had gone. 'A wish day without trouble with Martha – that would be too good to be true!'

CHAPTER 7

Robert the giant

'We were trying too hard,' said Cyril. 'That's why our wishes went wrong. Let's not think about wishes today. Let's play a game. While we are playing, a really good wish might come into someone's head.'

'All right,' said Anthea. 'Let's play bandits. But let's play in the sand pit. Then we will be near the sand fairy when we think of a wish.'

They collected Robert's bow and arrows, Jane's skipping rope, Martha's umbrella, and Father's old walking stick. (These were the swords.) They covered Baby's pram with a checked tablecloth. (This was the bandits' wagon – although Baby was fast asleep inside it.)

The game did not go well, and the children started to quarrel. Then Cyril saw the baker's boy. He was coming along the road with his basket full of bread.

'Stop!' cried Cyril, and he waved the umbrella at the baker's boy. 'Come and play.'

But he didn't want to play. He just pushed Cyril away.

Robert tripped the baker's boy up with the skipping rope, and he fell over. All the loaves of bread fell out of the basket, and rolled along the road.

'Why did you do that?' cried the baker's boy angrily. He stood up and brushed the dust from his clothes.

The baker's boy was much bigger than Robert. Robert looked up at his angry face, and started to run. The baker's boy chased Robert to the sand pit, and then went back to pick up the loaves of bread.

Sitting on the sand, Robert wiped away his tears.

'He's much bigger than I am!' he sniffed. 'That's why I ran away. I wish *I* was bigger than *he* is!'

He dug his fingers into the sand. He felt something furry, and jumped to his feet. It was the sand fairy, puffing himself up.

And Robert started to grow. Soon, he was bigger than the baker's boy. Much bigger. He was bigger than two men.

'We'd better ask for another wish!' said Anthea. 'We must make Robert go back to his normal size!'

But the sand fairy wouldn't help. And he disappeared into the sand.

'What shall we do now?' wailed Jane.

'I know what *I'm* going to do!' said Robert. 'I'm going to go after that baker's boy!'

And in three giant steps, he was back on the road. He hid behind a cottage, and waited for the baker's boy.

After a while, he heard someone whistling. He peered round the wall of the cottage. There was the baker's boy, carrying his basket.

Giant Robert jumped out, and grabbed the boy's collar.

'How dare you chase a boy who is smaller than you?' he boomed. (His voice was much louder now, too.)

He picked up the baker's boy, and put him on the roof of the cottage. 'You don't look so big now!' he cried.

Anthea asked Martha if they could have their lunch in the garden. (Robert was much too big to fit in the house.) Of course, Martha didn't notice Robert's size. She gave him his usual amount of meat and potatoes, and no more.

'There's a fair in the village,' Martha said, as she served the plum pie. 'My friend's going this afternoon.'

'*I'd* like to go to the fair,' said Robert, when Martha had gone.

'*You* can't go!' said Cyril. 'Giants don't go to fairs!'

'Oh!' cried Jane, and almost choked on a plum stone. 'I've got an idea! Listen – giants *do* go to fairs! People will pay money to see them! Let's take Robert to the fair!'

Robert didn't like the idea – until Anthea said, 'We couldn't do it without you, Robert. You can have most of the money.'

In the end, Robert took *them* to the fair. They climbed into an old pony cart, and Robert pulled it along. (This was easy for a giant.)

When they reached the village, Robert hid in a barn, and the others went into the fair. There were swings shaped like boats, and brightly painted roundabouts, and lots of other exciting things, but the children didn't stop to try them.

Cyril stopped at a coconut shy. He walked up to a lady in a red and white scarf, who was sorting out a pile of coconuts.

'Excuse me,' he said. 'I want to speak to the owner of this fair.'

'That's my husband, Bill. But he's asleep,' said the lady. She pointed to a red-faced man who lay under a tree. He was snoring loudly. 'I'm Becca. What's this all about?'

'I've got a giant,' said Cyril. 'He's in that barn. He could make a lot of money for you.'

'I'll have a look at him. But if this is a trick …'

Becca followed Cyril to the barn. He opened the door, and called out, 'Robert!'

A huge arm poked out of a pile of hay.

Becca's eyes were as big as saucers.

'My goodness!' she whispered.

A giant foot, and a leg, followed the arm. Then Giant Robert sat up, brushing off bits of hay.

'How much will you take for him?' asked Becca. Her eyes were as big as dinner plates now. 'He'll have the best of everything. I've got a lovely old caravan – an elephant used to live in it.'

'*He* won't take anything!' interrupted Robert. 'But *I* will take fifteen shillings.'

'Agreed!' smiled Becca, and handed him the money. 'Now come and meet Bill.'

Bill was very pleased with Robert and took him to a tent. It was very big, but Robert couldn't stand up in it.

Becca brought him some bread and cheese. Then Bill put a table in front of the tent, and stood on it.

'Ladies and gentlemen!' he cried. 'Come and see the biggest giant in the world! Three pence a go!'

Soon, a long line of people stood outside the tent. The children could hear 'Ooh!' and 'Aah!' – and sometimes a loud shriek.

At three o'clock, Robert said he wanted a cup of tea. Bill put up a notice:

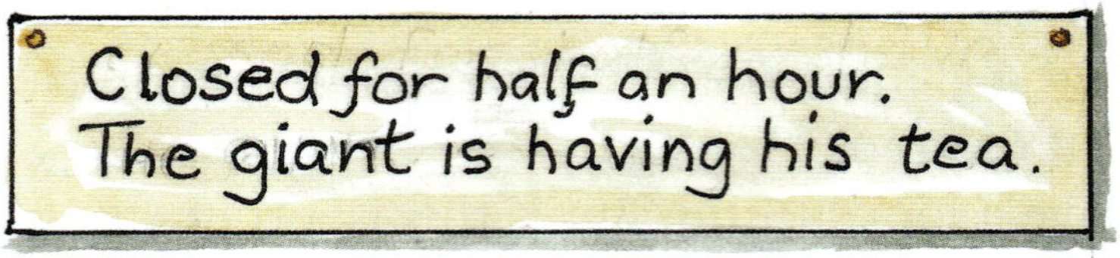

The children went into the tent to talk to Robert.

'How am I going to get away?' he asked them. 'They mustn't see me after sunset – I will be my normal size!'

Cyril thought for a moment. Then he went to find Bill.

'When the sun sets,' he began, 'the giant must be left alone. He gets very bad-tempered, you see. And a bad-tempered giant can make a lot of trouble.'

So just before sunset, another notice went up:

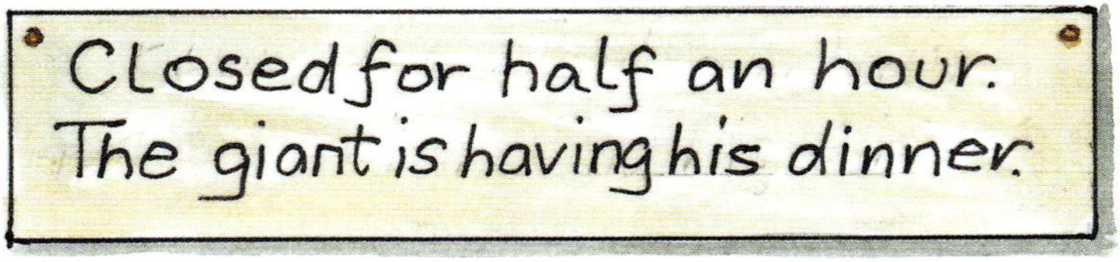

'There's one more thing,' said Cyril. 'He says that he's too hot. Will you open the tent up at the back – to give him some fresh air? Then I'll go and fetch his dinner.'

'All right,' said Bill. 'I'll be on guard at the front of the tent. Becca can stand at the back. Someone might try to steal our giant.'

Cyril sent his sisters home. In the tent, he told Robert the rest of his plan, and they settled down to wait.

One minute after sunset, a boy walked out of the front of the tent.

'I'm going to get the giant's dinner,' Cyril told Bill.

At the same time, a boy walked out of the back of the tent.

'I'm going to get the giant's dinner,' Robert told Becca.

And the two boys ran all the way home, laughing about the trick they had played.

CHAPTER 8

Baby grows up

The next morning, Cyril went to see the sand fairy. 'I've had an idea,' he said. 'We always come to the sand pit to make our wishes. And we can never decide what to wish for. Can we try wishing at home, or when we are out playing? Those wishes might be more sensible.'

The sand fairy stretched his furry brown arms, and yawned.

'Yes, you can,' he said sleepily, and disappeared into the sand.

It was a lovely sunny day, and the children decided to go into the woods to pick some nuts. After a while, they sat down on the mossy grass to rest.

But Baby didn't want to rest.

He pulled up handfuls of moss, and threw them at his brothers and sisters.

He took Cyril's watch out of his pocket, and tried to dig with it.

He trod on the watch, and broke the glass.

'Babies are babies for such a long time!' sighed Cyril. 'I can't wait for him to grow up!'

'He will grow up one day,' said Anthea dreamily, stroking Baby's hair.

'But *when*? He's so naughty! I wish he would grow up *now*!'

Anthea, Robert and Jane stared at Cyril.

'What have you done?' whispered Anthea.

And Baby started to change. First, his face became thinner. Then his mouth became bigger – and a little moustache appeared on his upper lip!

Anthea and Jane were horrified. They wished as hard as they could that the wish would stop. But when they opened their eyes, they saw a tall young man, wearing a grey suit and a green tie. On his head was a straw hat.

He leaned against a tree and asked, 'How far is it to the station? I might go to London for the afternoon!'

Baby's brothers and sisters looked miserably at each other. What would happen to him at sunset?

'You can't do that!' cried Anthea. 'Come to Rochester with us!'

'I'm your big brother. I can do as I like,' said Baby. 'And now, I'd like to be alone. Go home – and don't wait up for me. I'll be home very late.'

'Let me and Robert come with you,' suggested Cyril. He was very worried now.

'I've changed my mind,' said Baby. 'I think I'll ride my bicycle to Rochester.'

Anthea took a pin from her pocket, and quietly handed it to Cyril. He tiptoed away and ran to the road.

A shiny new bicycle was leaning on a gate. Quickly, Cyril pushed the pin into both the tyres. The air hissed out of them, and the tyres soon went flat.

When the others arrived, Robert said, 'Oh, dear! Your tyres are flat!'

Anthea bent down to look. When she stood up, she showed Baby a sharp thorn.

'So that's what did it!' said Baby. 'I'll need some water to help me mend the punctures.'

They went to look for some water. After a while, they saw a café.

The lady in the café gave them a bowl of water. Baby mended his punctures, and the others ate cheese sandwiches and chocolate cake.

When he had mended his punctures, Baby stood up.

He said, 'I can see a young lady! She's got a bicycle. A tyre on *her* bicycle is flat, too. I'll help her to mend it. Go home, all of you.'

The children didn't go home. They went to hide in the garden.

After a few moments, they heard Baby say, very politely, 'Have you got a puncture, Miss? I'd be very happy to mend it for you.'

'You are very kind,' replied the young lady.

When the puncture was mended, Baby said, 'It's getting late. May I ride with you?'

Anthea rushed out from her hiding place, and cried, 'Don't let him go with you! He's not what you think he is!'

'What do you mean?' she asked. 'What is he?'

'He's really just a baby! Or he will be when the sun sets.'

The young lady stared at Anthea. She thought Anthea was mad! She got on her bicycle and rode away.

When she had gone, Cyril spoke seriously to Baby.

'Let us take you home now,' he said. 'Things will look better in the morning.'

'You're all mad! Especially young Anthea,' replied Baby, looking puzzled. 'There's nothing wrong with me! I think *I'd* better take *you* home.'

While Baby wasn't looking, Robert had pushed the pin into one of Baby's tyres again. The bicycle now had another puncture, and Baby agreed to push it home.

They reached the White House just before sunset. Baby marched through the gate, and was met by Martha.

'Come to me, my darling Baby!' she cried, and picked him up.

Of course, to Martha, Baby looked the same as always. But the children saw a nursemaid carrying a tall young man in a grey suit and a green tie. He had a straw hat on his head – and a very cross expression on his face.

Later, when Baby was a baby again, Cyril said, 'What a dreadful young man! I hope Baby doesn't really grow up like that.'

'He won't,' said Anthea, stroking Baby's cheek. 'We will make sure of that.'

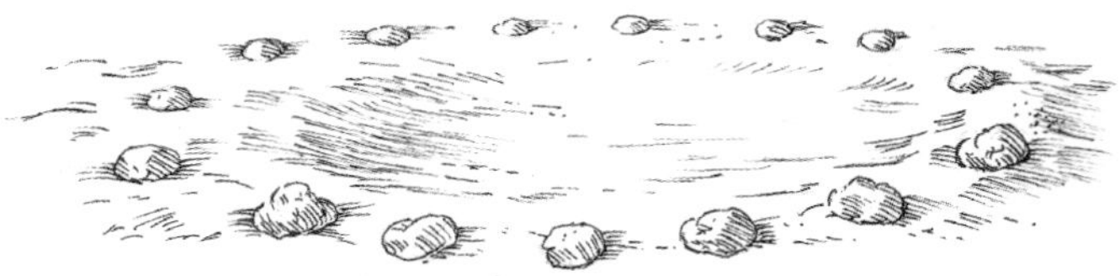

CHAPTER 9

Indians

Cyril was reading a book about cowboys and Indians. At breakfast the next morning, he said, 'I wish there were some Indians in the garden. Then we could all play cowboys and Indians. We could be the cowboys.'

'I don't think that's a very good idea,' said Anthea. 'It's the sort of wish that could go wrong.'

'That's true,' said Robert. 'Let's wish for money. Not gold coins, like last time. Let's wish for a hundred pounds.'

The others agreed, and they set off for the sand pit.

But when they told the sand fairy their wish, he was quite cross.

'You've had today's wish! Have you forgotten? You can make wishes anywhere now. You don't have to be here. You've already made a wish this morning.'

'What did we wish for?' asked Robert. He frowned as he tried to remember.

'You'll soon find out!' laughed the sand fairy, and he disappeared into the sand.

All morning, they tried to remember the wish. Then Jane found Cyril's book behind a chair.

'Oh, no!' she wailed. 'I remember now! Cyril wished for Indians!'

'Real Indians!' said Cyril. 'We might have to fight them!'

Anthea thought for a moment. Then she said, 'The important thing is to keep Baby out of danger. Come with me, Jane. I've got an idea.'

Jane followed her sister into Mother's bedroom. There was a big glass jug on the table, and Anthea carefully picked it up. She carried it into the bathroom, held it up in the air – and dropped it onto the stone floor.

Crash!

'Why did you do that?' gasped Jane.

'You'll see,' said Anthea.

Then Martha rushed up the stairs.

'What was that noise?' she said. 'What have you broken now?'

'I've broken Mother's jug,' said Anthea sadly. 'She loved it. I must buy her a new one. Will you go into Rochester for me, Martha? You could take Baby. Don't worry – I've got enough money for a new jug.'

'You just want to get rid of Baby for the afternoon!' said Martha.

'Please, Martha!' said Anthea.

'All right,' said Martha. 'But you must all be good while we are out.'

When Martha and Baby had gone, Cyril looked out of the window and said, 'I don't think the Indians will come now. It's almost three o'clock – oh, look!'

They all looked out of the window. A young man was peeping in at them! He had a painted face, and two feathers poked out of his long, black hair.

'They're here!' whispered Anthea. 'I knew it!'

The children ran round the house, looking out of the windows. They couldn't find any more Indians.

'They must be hiding in the trees!' gasped Robert. 'What are we going to do?'

'Let's dress up as Indians,' said Anthea. 'We'll try to frighten the real Indians. Robert, go and get some feathers from the hen house.'

Anthea went to get some blankets and scarves from the nursery. Jane found some black paper, to make their hair. Cyril fetched his paintbox, to paint their faces.

Anthea tied a white towel to Father's old walking stick. 'This is a white flag,' she explained. 'It means we want to make peace.'

The four Indians were soon ready to face the enemy. As they went out into the garden, Cook screamed with fright.

'Don't worry. It's only a game,' said Anthea. *We must look very frightening,* she thought.

Behind the hedge, they saw a row of feathers. Anthea stepped forward. She held up the white flag. One of the real Indians came to meet her.

'My name is Chief Golden Eagle!' he said.

'And I am – I am – Chief Black Panther!' said Anthea, thinking quickly.

'There are many of us,' Golden Eagle went on. 'If we fight, you will lose. Go back to your own land.'

'We will not,' said Anthea. 'We will fight you!'

Golden Eagle's men were coming closer. They carried bows and arrows, and axes.

'It's no good,' whispered Robert. 'Let's go back!'

But Anthea started to run towards the enemy.

The others followed her. A few Indians fell over, but the children kept on running – to the sand pit.

But the sand fairy wasn't there. And Golden Eagle's men were not far behind them.

Soon, the frightened children were surrounded by Indians. Their knives were gleaming in the sun.

'Make a fire!' ordered Golden Eagle, and ten of his men went to look for wood.

But they came back empty-handed.

'We can't find any wood, great leader,' said one man.

'No wood?' Golden Eagle was angry. 'No wood, to make a fire to burn our enemies? This is a strange country. I wish we were back in our own land!'

There was a flash of light – and the Indians disappeared!

The sand fairy had been there all the time. And he had granted Golden Eagle's wish.

When Martha came back with Baby, she was carrying a big glass jug. It looked exactly like the broken one.

'Here you are,' she said to Anthea. 'And here's your money, too. My sister gave me this jug, so I didn't need to buy one.'

'Thank you, Martha!' cried Anthea. She put her arms round Martha's neck and hugged her.

'Hug me while you can,' said Martha. 'When your mother comes back, I'm going to tell her I'm leaving.'

'Martha!' gasped Anthea. 'Are you leaving because we've been naughty?'

'No,' smiled Martha. 'I'm leaving because – I'm going to get married!'

CHAPTER 10

The last wish

The next morning, a letter from Mother arrived. Grandmother was much better, and Mother would be back at the White House that afternoon. The children were very happy.

'Today's wish must be something for Mother,' said Cyril. 'What would she like, do you think?'

'She would like us to be good,' said Jane. 'She often wishes for that.'

'Yes, but we can be good without help from the sand fairy,' said Cyril.

Then Martha came in with a pot of tea.

'Something terrible has happened!' she said. 'Someone has stolen all Lady Chittenden's jewellery! Her pearl necklaces, her diamond rings and her gold bracelets!'

'Lady Chittenden?' said Anthea. 'We know her! She lives in a very grand house, and she wears a red and white dress!'

'That's her,' said Martha. 'And she's very upset. Her jewellery was worth thousands of pounds. Now, I must clean this house before your mother arrives.'

When Martha had gone, Anthea said, 'I didn't like Lady Chittenden very much. She is so rich. Our mother only has two rings and a little pearl brooch – and she's got no diamonds at all!'

'When I'm a famous explorer, I'll buy her *lots* of diamonds,' said Robert.

'Wouldn't it be lovely ...' Jane said dreamily, 'if Mother found Lady Chittenden's jewellery – in her room? Oh, I wish she would!'

Robert stared at her.

'Jane! Why did you wish that?' he asked. 'The wish will come true! Then we'll be taken to the police station again, and Mother and Father will be so angry ...'

'We must find the jewellery,' decided Cyril, 'and take it back to Lady Chittenden.'

They went upstairs to Mother's room, and started to look for the jewellery. They looked on the dressing table, and in the chest of drawers, and under the bed, and on top of the wardrobe. But they couldn't find anything.

'I know why we can't find the jewellery,' said Robert. '*Mother* has to find it – that was what Jane wished for.'

'We'll have to tell Mother the truth,' said Anthea. 'We'll tell her all about the sand fairy and the wishes, and she'll give back the jewellery – and everything will be all right!'

'Do you think so?' asked Cyril. 'I don't think she would believe us. Would you believe in a sand fairy, if you had never seen one? She will think we're making it up.'

'Cyril's right,' said Anthea. 'A grown-up wouldn't believe in a sand fairy. But there's nothing we can do about it. So let's fill the house with flowers, and get ready to welcome Mother home.'

So they picked lots of red roses, and put them around the house in pots and jars.

Mother arrived after lunch, and was very pleased with the roses. They had lots of things to talk about, and the children almost forgot about the sand fairy and the wish.

But then Mother said, 'I need to take off my hat and unpack my case. I'm going up to my room now.'

'Oh, don't go to your room!' cried Anthea. 'I'll take your things upstairs for you!'

'No – I need to wash my hands and comb my hair.'

The children slowly followed their mother upstairs. She took off her hat and washed her hands. Then she went to her dressing table to comb her hair.

'Oh! What's this?' she asked. She picked up a small leather box. She opened it, and took out a glittering ring. 'Pearls and diamonds! How lovely! Father must have sent it for me. I'll go and ask Martha.'

Of course, Martha knew nothing about the ring.

'It's a mystery!' smiled Mother. She put the ring on her finger. It sparkled in the light.

Then she opened her drawer to take out her comb, and she found a diamond necklace.

When she went to put her hat in the wardrobe, she found a gold brooch.

And the more she looked, the more jewellery she found.

Mother was not smiling now. Jane started to cry.

'You know something about this, Jane,' said Mother. 'Now tell me the truth.'

'We – we found a fairy, in the sand pit,' said poor Jane.

'Don't be silly, Jane! Tell me the truth, please!'

Cyril said, 'We've never seen the jewellery before! But we know that burglars took all Lady Chittenden's jewellery last night. Maybe they hid it here, in your room!'

'Why would they do that? I'm going to the police.' Mother put her hat back on. 'Don't let anyone into the house.'

'What now?' said Jane, when Mother had gone.

'We can't wait until sunset,' said Anthea. 'We'll have to go to the sand fairy. If we beg him, he might give us another wish. Come on, Jane.'

The sand fairy was washing his whiskers in the sun.

'You again!' he said. 'I suppose you want another wish. Can't I have any time to myself?'

'Dear, kind sand fairy!' said Anthea. 'Please give us one more wish – and we will never ask again!'

'Do you mean it? I am so tired!'

'Yes,' said Anthea. 'I wish that Lady Chittenden had not been burgled.'

'Done!' said the sand fairy. 'Anything else?'

Jane said, 'I wish that Mother would forget all about the jewellery.'

'Done! Now, will you make a wish for *me*?'

'Can't you make wishes for yourself?'

'Oh, no. Now – my wish is that you never tell a grown-up about me.'

'Why?'

'Because then I would have no peace at all! Grown-ups would wish for all sorts of silly things.'

Anthea made the wish, and the sand fairy puffed himself out again.

'Thank you for everything,' said Anthea. 'I hope you have a good long sleep. And I hope we see you again.'

'Is that a wish?' asked the sand fairy, drowsily.

'Yes! It's our very last one!'

Back at the White House, Martha said, 'You'll never guess! Lady Chittenden wasn't burgled after all! She sent her jewellery away to be cleaned – and then forgot all about it!'

The children looked at each other, and smiled.

Then Mother came in.

'I went into Rochester to buy your school dresses,' she said. 'Will you ask Martha for a pot of tea, please, Anthea?'

'She *has* forgotten!' whispered Jane to the boys.

While Mother put Baby to bed, the four children sat in the garden.

'I wonder if we *will* ever see the sand fairy again,' said Jane.

'That was our very last wish,' said Anthea. 'I'm sure it will come true.'

The children *did* see the sand fairy again. But that, of course, is another story.

Farewell to the farm

The coach is at the door at last;
The eager children, mounting fast
And kissing hands, in chorus sing:
Goodbye, goodbye, to everything!

To house and garden, field and lawn,
The meadow gates we swung upon,
To pump and stable, tree and swing,
Goodbye, goodbye, to everything!

And fare you well for ever more,
O ladder at the hayloft door,
O hayloft where the cobwebs cling,
Goodbye, goodbye, to everything!

Crack goes the whip, and off we go;
The trees and houses smaller grow;
Last, round the woody turn we swing:
Goodbye, goodbye, to everything!

Robert Louis Stevenson

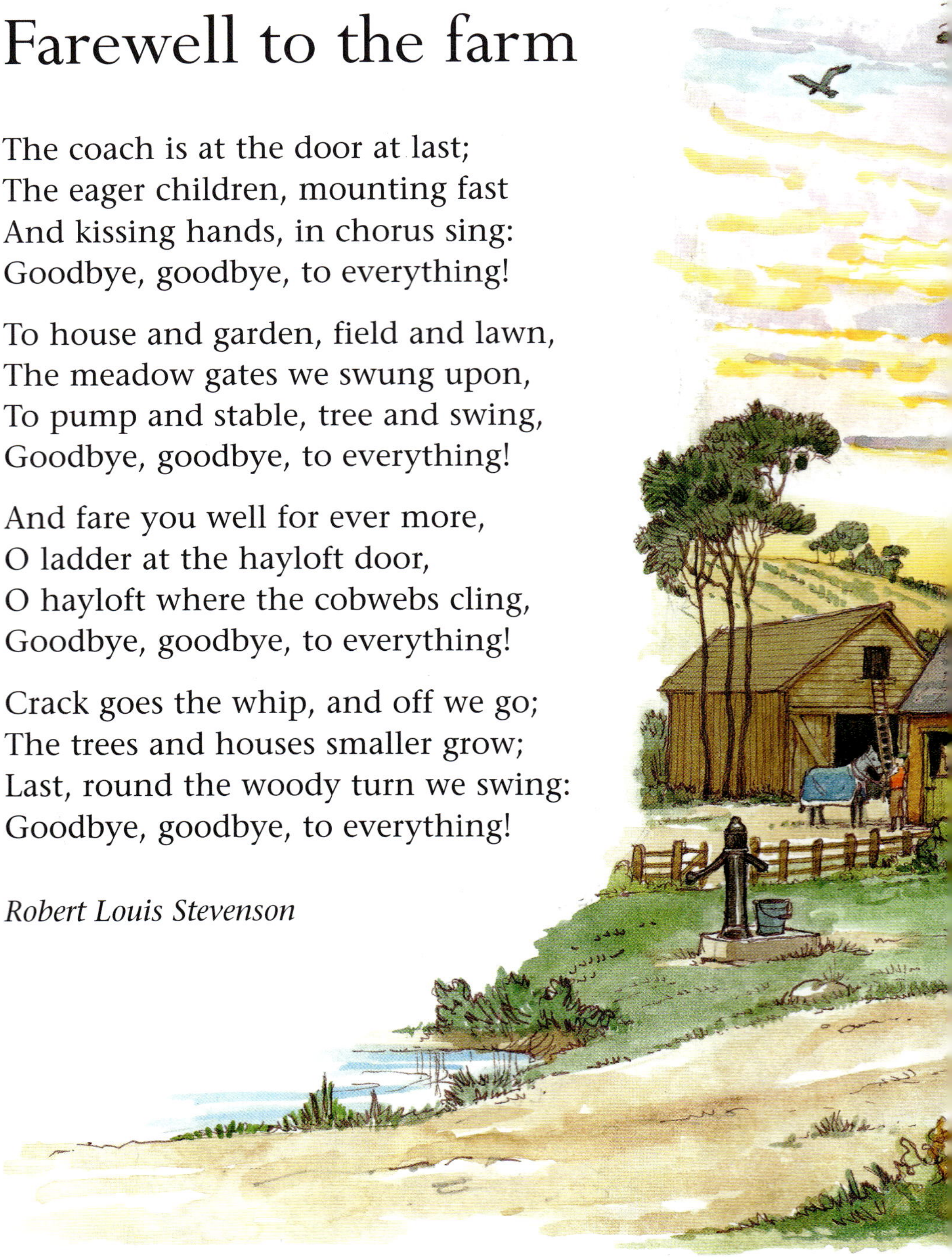

Living in the 1900s

The children in the story lived in the 1900s. Life in Britain was very different then.

- There was no electricity for heating, keeping food cool, cooking or lighting.
- There was no running water for washing and cleaning the house, and there was no washing machine for doing the laundry.
- There was no radio or television, and there were no computers, CDs or telephones.
- Many families had servants to help with the cooking and the housework.

Cooking

Food was cooked on a cooker called a range. The range was heated by a coal fire.

There were no refrigerators, and fresh food was kept in a cool, dark room called a pantry.

Heating and lighting

Houses were heated by coal fires.

The living rooms were lit by oil lamps, and people took candles to bed with them.

Washing

Water was fetched from a pump outside the house. The water was heated on the range, and taken to each bedroom in a jug. Then it was poured into a bowl so people could wash themselves.

Once a week, people had a bath and washed their hair. Water was heated in a big heater called a copper, and poured into a tin bath. The bath was stood near the fire to keep the water warm.

There were no flush lavatories, and people kept pots called chamber pots under their beds. Most houses had an outdoor lavatory.

Laundry

Clothes were washed in a big tub. The water was heated in the copper. The clothes were stirred with a stick to get the dirt out.

The water was squeezed out of the clothes in a machine called a mangle. Two wooden rollers were turned by a handle.

The clothes were hung up to dry on a washing line in the garden. If it was raining, they were hung up in front of the fire.

To iron the clothes, flat irons were used. These were the same shape as electric irons, but they had to be heated on the range.

About the author – Edith Nesbit

Edith Nesbit was born in London in 1858. She was the youngest of four children. When the children were young, the Nesbit family travelled around France. Edith loved reading, and she spent much of her time with her nose in a book.

The family settled in Kent, just outside London, and Edith started to write poetry. When she was only fifteen, some of her poems were printed in a magazine.

When Edith was twenty-one, she married a man called Hubert Bland, who worked in a bank. They had three children.

Edith didn't become famous for her children's stories until she was forty years old. She liked to use the initial 'E', so that readers couldn't tell if she was a man or a woman.

Hubert Bland died in 1914, and in the same year the First World War broke out. During the war, Edith sold fruit and flowers to make some money. She married again in 1917.

Edith Nesbit died in Kent in 1924.

Macmillan Education
4 Crinan Street
London N1 9XW
A division of Springer Nature Limited
Companies and representatives throughout the world

ISBN-13 978-1-4050-6021-9

First published 2007

Design and layout by Anthony Godber
Illustrated by Kay Dixey
Cover design by Linda Reed & Associates
Cover illustration by Kay Dixey

The Series Editor and the Author would like to give special thanks to Gill McLean for her contribution in setting up the *Macmillan Explorers* series, for her continuous encouragement, and for her positive and practical help and advice throughout its production.

The authors and publishers would like to thank the following for permission to reproduce their photographic material:
Alamy/ David Bagley p77; Corbis/Bettmann p74;
Getty Images/Hulton Archive p75;
Topfoto/Topham Picturepoint p78.

Printed and bound in Dubai

2022 2021 2020 2019 2018
21 20 19 18 17 16